MEGABUGS

And Other Prehistoric Critters That Roamed the Planet

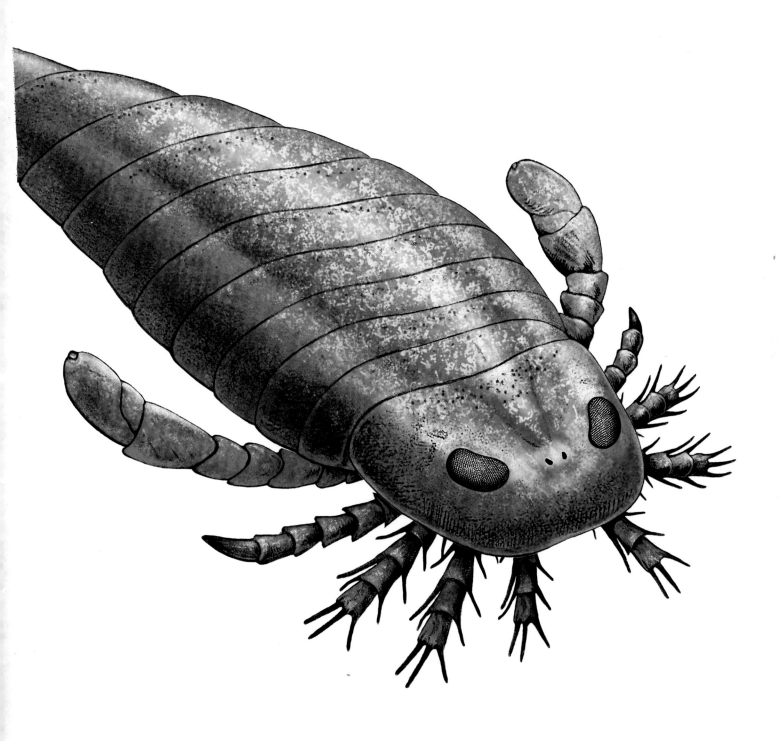

MEGABUGS

And Other Prehistoric Critters That Roamed the Planet

Written by
Helaine Becker

Illustrated by
John Bindon

KIDS CAN PRESS

For Mom and Dad — H.B.

Many thanks to Jason, Peter and Tom for their invaluable insights
that helped me bring to life these wonderful creatures — J.B.

ACKNOWLEDGMENTS

Many thanks to Dr. Carsten Brauckmann from the Institute of Geology and Palaeontology at
the Clausthal University of Technology for his review of the manuscript. He provided many
helpful suggestions to ensure the text's factual accuracy. As well, thank you to DoEun Kwon
for her help in researching the appearances of the animals in the book.

Kids Can Press gratefully acknowledges the financial support of the Government of Ontario,
through Ontario Creates; the Ontario Arts Council; the Canada Council for the Arts;
and the Government of Canada for our publishing activity.

Published in Canada and the U.S. by Kids Can Press Ltd.
25 Dockside Drive, Toronto, ON M5A 0B5

Kids Can Press is a Corus Entertainment Inc. company

www.kidscanpress.com

The artwork in this book was rendered in pencil and line then finalized and colored digitally.
The text is set in Univers LT Std and FlingaLing.

Edited by Katie Scott and Stacey Roderick
Designed by Michael Reis

Printed and bound in Shenzhen, China, in 3/2019 by C & C Offset

CM 19 0 9 8 7 6 5 4 3 2 1

Library and Archives Canada Cataloguing in Publication

Becker, Helaine, author
Megabugs / written by Helaine Becker ; illustrated by John Bindon.

Includes index.
ISBN 978-1-77138-811-5 (hardcover)

1. Arthropoda, Fossil — Juvenile literature. 2. Insects, Fossil — Juvenile
literature. I. Bindon, John, illustrator II. Title.

QE815.B43 2019   j565   C2018-906102-2

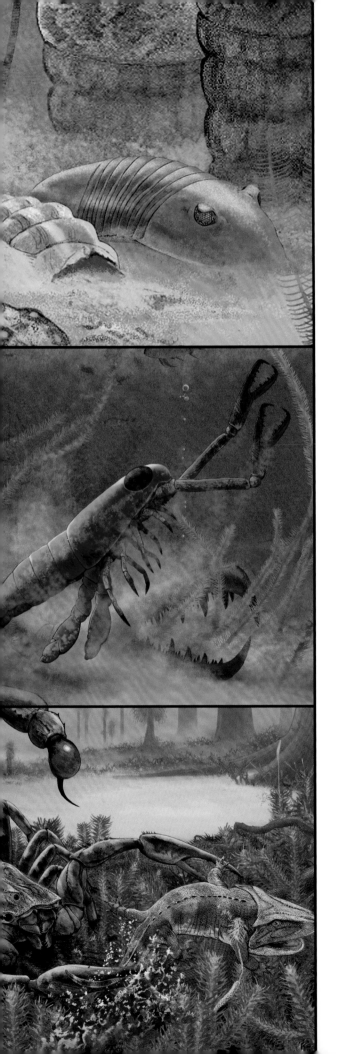

Contents

IMAGINE, DEEP IN THE JUNGLE ...

A swift-moving millipede almost twice your size slithers toward you, snapping its slavering jaws. Nearby, a pit bull–sized scorpion jabs its venom-tipped tail at an unfortunate passerby.

Megabugs — supersized, insect-like critters — may seem like the stuff of nightmares. But they once dominated our planet, long before humans came on the scene. They were the very real ancestors of modern-day insects, spiders, crabs and other arthropods.

In this peek into prehistory, you'll meet many of these horrifying creatures. You'll find out how they lived. You'll find out why they grew so big. And you'll find out what (thankfully) caused their extinction. Plus, you'll discover some megabugs that still roam the earth today!

What's an Arthropod?

All of the critters in this book are arthropods. Today, this group of animals includes:

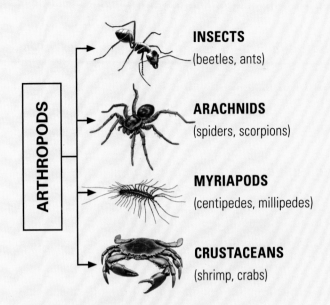

ARTHROPODS

INSECTS
(beetles, ants)

ARACHNIDS
(spiders, scorpions)

MYRIAPODS
(centipedes, millipedes)

CRUSTACEANS
(shrimp, crabs)

How Can You Recognize an Arthropod?

Arthropods are invertebrates (animals without a backbone) with a few telltale features:

■ **SEGMENTED BODY:**

a body with more than one part. For example, insect bodies have three main parts: a head, a thorax and an abdomen.

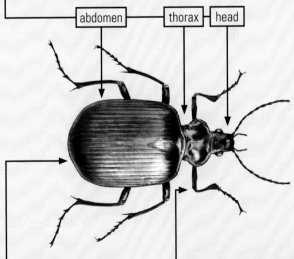

abdomen — thorax — head

■ **EXOSKELETON:**

a hard outer shell (outside skeleton) that protects the body. All arthropods molt (shed their exoskeleton). A new exoskeleton grows in its place.

■ **JOINTED APPENDAGES:**

at least six jointed legs (*arthropod* means "jointed foot") and, often, two antennae for sensing their surroundings.

HOW OLD IS EARTH?

Using a measuring technique called radiometric dating, scientists can pinpoint how long ago any rock was formed. By measuring and comparing rocks from all over the world (and even from the moon!), scientists know that Earth is more than 4.54 billion years old.

To help make sense of all that history, we divide it into time frames called eras. Each era is further broken down into periods. The megabugs you'll encounter throughout these pages are all from the Paleozoic era.

EARTH IS ALWAYS CHANGING

To this day, the planet continues to change. Continents slowly grow, merge, disappear or move apart. Volcanoes erupt, causing new land to appear. Temperatures rise and fall. When Earth changes, so do the living things that call it home. What will this mean for all living things on Earth today? Only time will tell.

PRECAMBRIAN — 4,540–542

CAMBRIAN PERIOD
Animals exist only in the ocean — 542–488

ORDOVICIAN PERIOD
First vertebrates (animals with a backbone) appear — 488–444

SILURIAN PERIOD
First air-breathing animals appear — 444–416

DEVONIAN PERIOD
First insects and amphibians appear — 416–359

CARBONIFEROUS PERIOD
Animals now thrive on land; first reptiles appear — 359–299

PERMIAN PERIOD
First ancestors of mammals and dinosaurs appear — 299–251

PALEOZOIC ERA

Mass extinction kills about 90 percent of life on Earth

TRIASSIC PERIOD
First dinosaurs and mammals appear — 251–200

JURASSIC PERIOD
First birds appear — 200–145

CRETACEOUS PERIOD
First marsupials appear — 145–66

MESOZOIC ERA

Mass extinction kills 75 percent of plants and animals

PALEOGENE PERIOD
First primates (ancestors to humans) and rodents appear — 66–23

NEOGENE PERIOD
Animals start to resemble their modern forms — 23–3

QUATERNARY PERIOD
First humans appear — 3–TODAY

CENOZOIC ERA

MILLIONS OF YEARS AGO

THE DANGLER

Plankton was Aegirocassis's favorite snack. It is made up of tiny plants, animals and microorganisms that drift through the water or float on its surface.

Aegirocassis *480–478 million years ago*

Paleozoic era
542–251 million years ago

Cambrian period

Ordovician period
488–444 million years ago

Silurian period

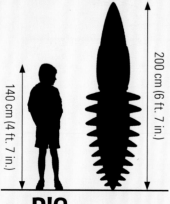

140 cm (4 ft. 7 in.)

200 cm (6 ft. 7 in.)

HOW **BIG** COULD IT GROW?

Aegirocassis *(EE-gear-o-KA-sis)*

Name Meaning: giant ruler of the seas

Number of Species: 1

Habitat: ocean

Fave Snack: plankton

Survival Strategy: "the lazy fisher"

Modern Relatives: arthropods

Fossils Found:

Morocco

ADAPTATION

All living things need a survival strategy. They need to find food, protect themselves from predators and the elements, and produce the next generation.

If a species couldn't compete for food anymore, it would have to change, or adapt. Otherwise, it would go extinct, just like Aegirocassis. Over a long period of time, an organism might adapt so much that it becomes an entirely new species. Adaptation has happened throughout Earth's history, causing billions of changes. And it's still happening today!

There's a reason why Aegirocassis is named after Aegir, a giant sea god in Norse mythology. This sea creature was twice the size of any other animal at the time.

Aegirocassis may have maintained its huge size as a defense against predators. As the biggest creature in the sea, it was too large for any other animal to swallow!

Like some species of modern-day whales, Aegirocassis was a filter feeder. It fed on plankton, the ocean's tiniest plants and animals. Sometimes it would have to swim to find plankton. Other times, it could just dangle in the water and wait for it to float by. Then its netlike front appendages would filter the plankton straight into its ginormous mouth.

Aegirocassis would have needed huge amounts of plankton to survive. Over time, more animals were likely competing for this food source — and there wasn't enough of it to go around. Aegirocassis's giant-sized body could not adapt. Eventually, it went extinct.

Isotelus would chow down on anything it could find: live prey, dead animals and even other trilobites!

Isotelus 472–444 million years ago

Paleozoic era
542–251 million years ago

Cambrian period

Ordovician period
488–444 million years ago

Silurian period

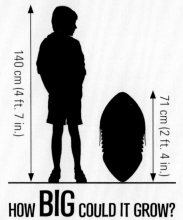

140 cm (4 ft. 7 in.)

71 cm (2 ft. 4 in.)

HOW **BIG** COULD IT GROW?

Isotelus *(EYE-so-TELL-us)*

Name Meaning: equal spear
Number of Species: 13
Habitat: ocean
Fave Snack: dead animals
Survival Strategy: "the creep 'n' crawl"
Modern Relatives: none

Fossils Found:

Canada   Norway   Estonia

U.S.A.

China

Greenland

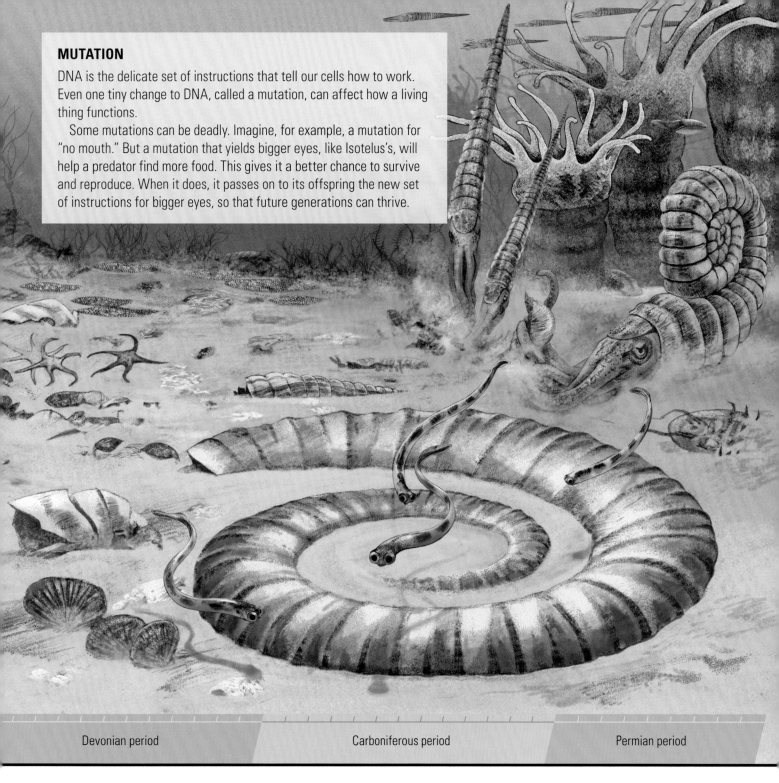

Devonian period	Carboniferous period	Permian period

Isotelus was a cockroach-like megabug that crept along the seabed. It was a bottom-feeder, meaning it ate animals and other organisms on the ocean floor. Its large compound eyes, with thousands of tiny lenses, could easily spy critters in its path. Then ... *chomp!*

Isotelus belonged to a group of arthropods called trilobites. These hard-shelled animals had mutations that made them both predators (animals that hunt live prey) and scavengers (animals that eat dead organisms).

Basically, trilobites would eat anything they could scarf down.

It's tempting to think that extinct animals like Isotelus were, somehow, failures. Not true. Isotelus thrived for more than 28 million years. So why did it go extinct? Some scientists think it was because of a sudden worldwide cooling at the end of the Ordovician period. The warmth-loving larvae could not survive long enough to reproduce in colder oceans. Eventually, there were too few adults to sustain the species.

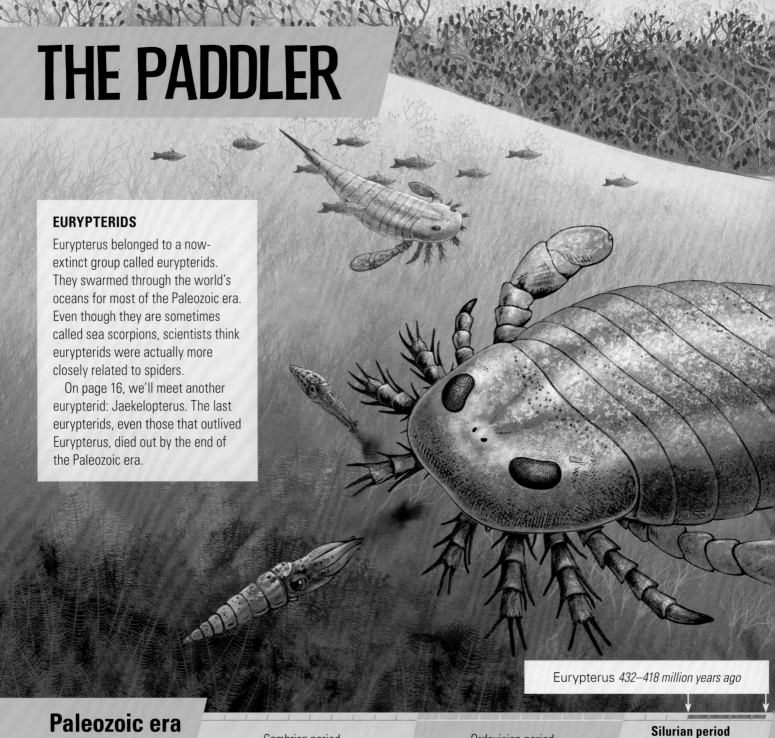

THE PADDLER

EURYPTERIDS

Eurypterus belonged to a now-extinct group called eurypterids. They swarmed through the world's oceans for most of the Paleozoic era. Even though they are sometimes called sea scorpions, scientists think eurypterids were actually more closely related to spiders.

On page 16, we'll meet another eurypterid: Jaekelopterus. The last eurypterids, even those that outlived Eurypterus, died out by the end of the Paleozoic era.

Eurypterus *432–418 million years ago*

Paleozoic era
542–251 million years ago

Cambrian period

Ordovician period

Silurian period
444–416 million years ago

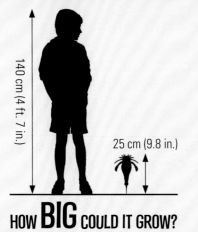

140 cm (4 ft. 7 in.)

25 cm (9.8 in.)

HOW **BIG** COULD IT GROW?

Eurypterus *(you-RIP-ter-us)*

Name Meaning: broad paddle

Number of Species: 16

Habitat: ocean

Fave Snack: cephalopods

Survival Strategy: "the stroll 'n' swim"

Modern Relatives: scorpions, king crabs and spiders

Fossils Found:

Canada

Norway

Estonia

U.S.A.

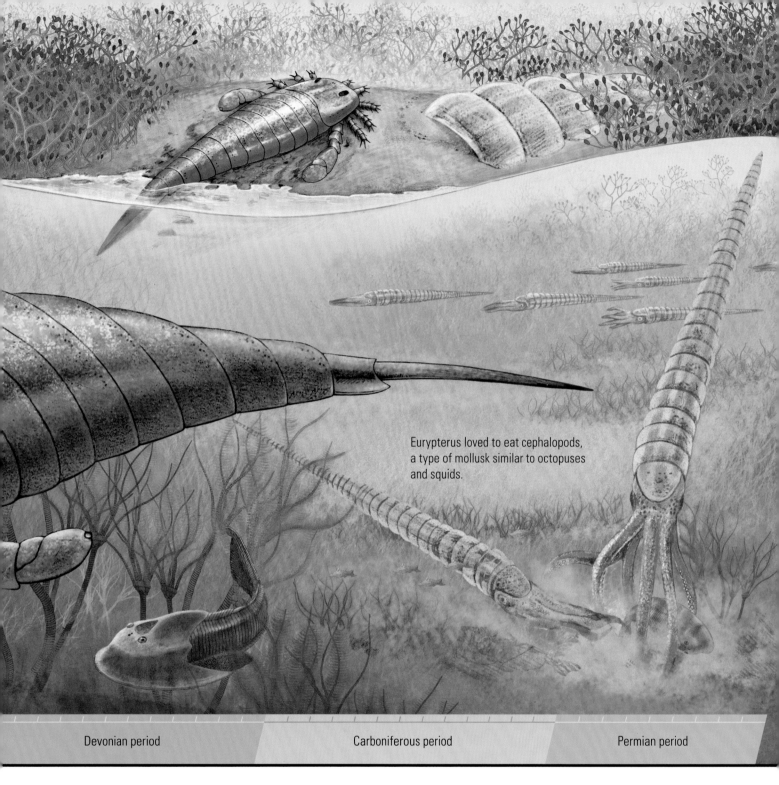

Eurypterus loved to eat cephalopods, a type of mollusk similar to octopuses and squids.

| Devonian period | Carboniferous period | Permian period |

Like modern scorpions, Eurypterus hunted using the sharp tip of its tail, called a telson, and two pincer-like mouthparts. This critter was about the size of a Chihuahua and might have adapted to a larger size so it could keep chomping on fish that had developed bony protective "armor."

And what if there were slim pickings on the shallow seafloor? Eurypterus was a great swimmer. One strong stroke of its paddle-like legs let it glide through water in search of its next meal.

Eurypterus had still another zinger in its survival toolbox. It was the first animal that could briefly walk on land! It probably left the sea to mate, lay eggs or escape predators — especially after molting (when its new exoskeleton was soft and vulnerable).

So why did Eurypterus go extinct? It might have faced too much competition for food from the many members of its group, the eurypterids.

THE STINGER

Pulmonoscorpius likely would have feasted on tetrapods: four-legged animals, such as amphibians and reptiles. (The word *tetrapod* means "four feet.")

Paleozoic era
542–251 million years ago

| Cambrian period | Ordovician period | Silurian period |

140 cm (4 ft. 7 in.)

79 cm (2 ft. 7 in.)

HOW **BIG** COULD IT GROW?

Pulmonoscorpius (pull-muh-no-SKOR-pee-us)

Name Meaning: breathing scorpion

Number of Species: 1

Habitat: forests and swamps

Fave Snack: possibly tetrapods

Survival Strategy: "the toxic stab"

Modern Relatives: scorpions

Fossils Found:

Scotland

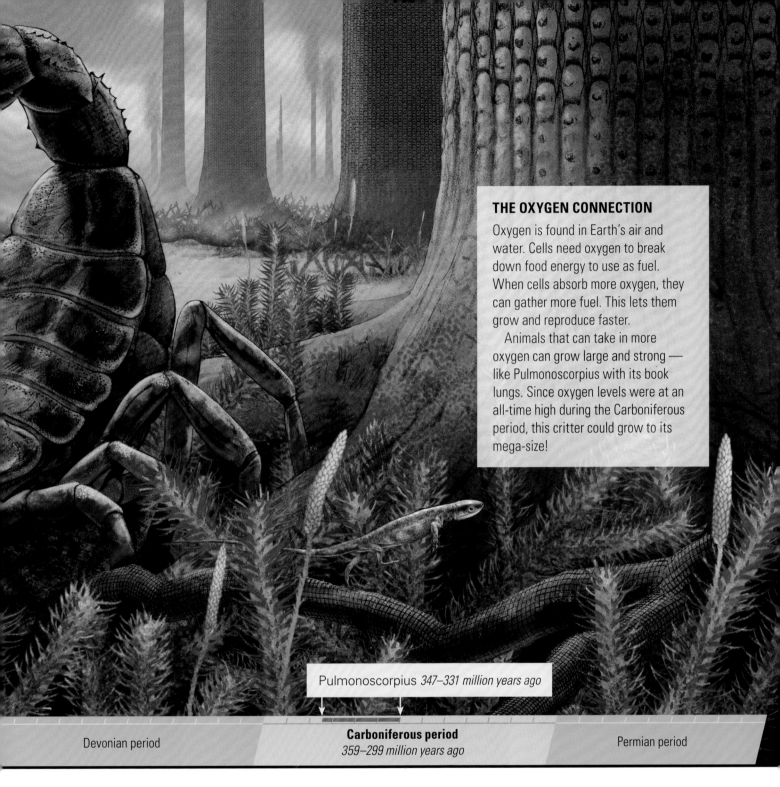

THE OXYGEN CONNECTION

Oxygen is found in Earth's air and water. Cells need oxygen to break down food energy to use as fuel. When cells absorb more oxygen, they can gather more fuel. This lets them grow and reproduce faster.

Animals that can take in more oxygen can grow large and strong — like Pulmonoscorpius with its book lungs. Since oxygen levels were at an all-time high during the Carboniferous period, this critter could grow to its mega-size!

Pulmonoscorpius *347–331 million years ago*

Devonian period

Carboniferous period
359–299 million years ago

Permian period

Imagine a scorpion the size of a pit bull. Pulmonoscorpius was that scary creature. It had huge, sharp pincers, and its telson could stab and paralyze prey with its venom. Then it would suck the fluids from inside the still-living body.

Pulmonoscorpius arrived on the scene during the Carboniferous period. By then, green plants had been growing on land for more than 150 million years. They released huge amounts of oxygen into the air. For the first time, animals could breathe and live entirely on land.

To take advantage of these new conditions, Pulmonoscorpius developed a new organ, called a book lung, to breathe oxygen from the air. (Previously, arthropods breathed underwater through gills, similar to how fish breathe.) The book lung had many layers of tissue, just like the pages of a book. Each layer could gather large amounts of oxygen, helping this eight-legged monster grow to a staggering size. Pulmonoscorpius may have gone extinct when climate change caused its swampy habitat to dry up.

THE SLITHERER

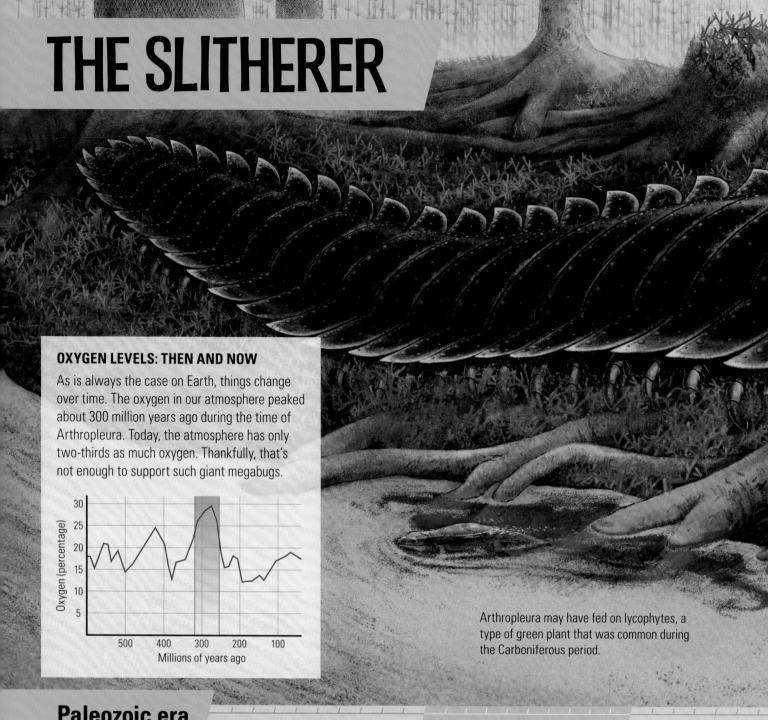

OXYGEN LEVELS: THEN AND NOW

As is always the case on Earth, things change over time. The oxygen in our atmosphere peaked about 300 million years ago during the time of Arthropleura. Today, the atmosphere has only two-thirds as much oxygen. Thankfully, that's not enough to support such giant megabugs.

Chart: Oxygen (percentage) vs. Millions of years ago
Y-axis: Oxygen (percentage) — 5, 10, 15, 20, 25, 30
X-axis: Millions of years ago — 500, 400, 300, 200, 100

Arthropleura may have fed on lycophytes, a type of green plant that was common during the Carboniferous period.

Paleozoic era
542–251 million years ago

Cambrian period | Ordovician period | Silurian period

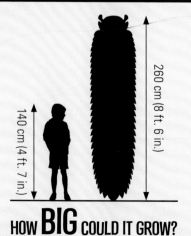

140 cm (4 ft. 7 in.)

260 cm (8 ft. 6 in.)

HOW BIG COULD IT GROW?

Arthropleura *(AR-throw-PLOO-ruh)*

Name Meaning: jointed rib

Number of Species: 6

Habitat: swamps and rain forests

Fave Snack: swamp plants

Survival Strategy: "the leg hold"

Modern Relatives: millipedes

Fossils Found:

the Netherlands
Scotland
Germany
France
Canada
U.S.A.

Arthropleura *330–290 million years ago*

Devonian period	**Carboniferous period** *359–299 million years ago*	Permian period

By the time Arthropleura slithered onto the scene, oxygen levels in the atmosphere had hit an all-time high. This colossal creeper was able to make good use of the rich oxygen to grow into a true giant. Millipede-like Arthropleura had up to 30 body segments (the "ribs" that gave it its name). They formed a long, slithery yet sturdy chain.

Arthropleura was the largest arthropod that ever lived. Growing up to 2.6 m (8 ft. 6 in.) long, it was bigger than a basketball player. And with up to 80 quick-moving, grasping legs, it could have easily gripped and smothered one, too!

No one knows for sure what Arthropleura ate. It crept through the swamps and tropical rain forests of the Carboniferous period, so it might have gulped up swampy plants. Either way, a plentiful food supply and few predators may have contributed to its gigantism. It died out as the climate gradually became drier.

Meganeuropsis probably feasted on insects called Palaeodictyoptera, which resembled giant mayflies.

Paleozoic era
542–251 million years ago

Cambrian period	Ordovician period	Silurian period

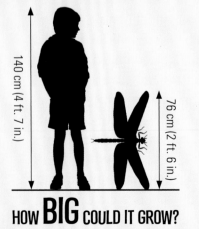

140 cm (4 ft. 7 in.)

76 cm (2 ft. 6 in.)

HOW **BIG** COULD IT GROW?

Meganeuropsis *(MEH-guh-ner-OP-sis)*

Name Meaning: big nerve

Number of Species: 2

Habitat: wetlands

Fave Snack: Palaeodictyoptera

Survival Strategy: "the swoop 'n' snatch"

Modern Relatives: dragonflies and damselflies

Fossils Found:

U.S.A.

Meganeuropsis *290 million years ago*

| Devonian period | Carboniferous period | **Permian period** *299–251 million years ago* |

In the Permian period, the air was still rich with oxygen. This would have helped bugs continue to grow large and even take to the skies! That's because oxygen is heavier than other gases in our atmosphere, such as hydrogen and nitrogen. Acting like a cushion, oxygen-rich air can support heavier — and bigger! — insects as they take off and stay aloft.

Meganeuropsis was the largest insect that ever lived. It belonged to a group of extinct insects called the griffinflies. It looked like a dragonfly but was almost 8.5 times larger. It was given its name because it had large nerves visible in its giant wings. We know this from its fossils.

You wouldn't want this hungry, meat-eating megabug to land on your shoulder. As a fully grown adult, it could snatch and crush prey in its toothed mandibles, or jaws. But despite its awesome survival skills, Meganeuropsis could not survive the changing climate.

GIANTS OF TODAY

Giant arthropods continued to live for millions of years after the Paleozoic era. The flea-like Pseudopulex (2.3 cm / 0.895 in.), about the size of your thumb, pestered the dinosaurs during the Mesozoic era. Titanomyrma, a supersized acid-spraying ant (14.9 cm / 5.9 in.), swarmed forest floors in the early Cenozoic era.

Big by today's standards, these megabugs couldn't hold a candle to the giants that had come before. That's because after the Carboniferous period, the atmosphere's oxygen levels started to drop. This made it harder for arthropods to grow to such mega-sizes. Thankfully, given the current oxygen levels in our atmosphere, this is mostly still the case.

Some giant arthropods, however, do exist today. Check out these contemporary megabugs.

COLOSSAL CRAB

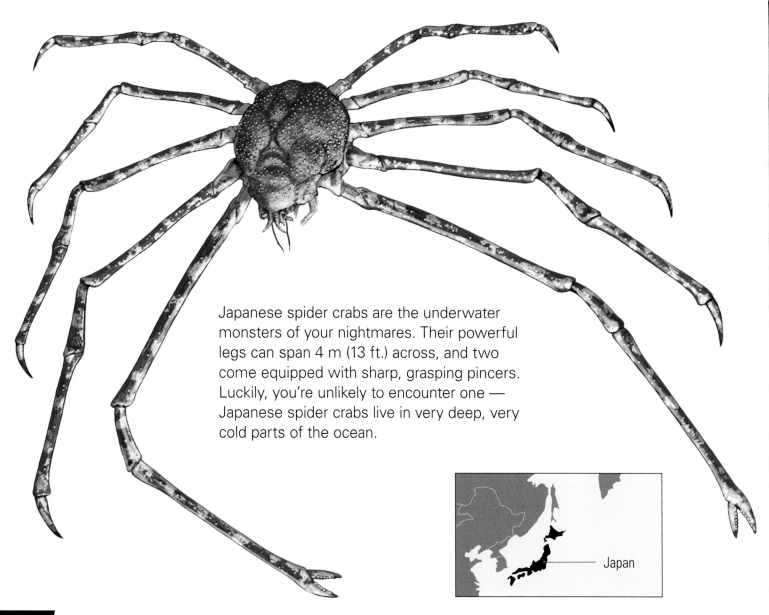

Japanese spider crabs are the underwater monsters of your nightmares. Their powerful legs can span 4 m (13 ft.) across, and two come equipped with sharp, grasping pincers. Luckily, you're unlikely to encounter one — Japanese spider crabs live in very deep, very cold parts of the ocean.

Japan

SUPERSIZED SPIDER

The giant huntsman is a species of super-speedy spider. It lives in Australia, and its leg span measures over 28 cm (11 in.). Despite its enormous size, its flattened body allows it to squeeze into small spaces to hunt for prey. It's also frighteningly fast — it can scuttle at speeds up to 1 m (3 ft.) a second!

Australia

REVOLTING ROACH

The giant burrowing cockroach is the largest cockroach that ever lived. It measures 7.6 cm (3 in.) long. Researchers have recently discovered its unique adaptation: smaller-than-normal respiratory organs. That leaves more space inside its body for the oxygen it needs to grow and thrive.

Australia

MEGABUGS OF THE FUTURE

In the billions of years since Earth formed, its climate and geography have varied enormously. Today, we are in a new period of great change. The atmosphere's carbon dioxide levels are increasing, and temperatures around the world are rising. How will these changes affect the next generation of insects? Only time will tell.

A Note on the Illustrations

The prehistoric critters in this book have been extinct for millions of years. So how do we know what they looked like? The fossils they left behind provide the best clues. They can show us the shapes and sizes of the animals, and sometimes even their colors. The illustrations in these pages were created based on research and fossil evidence, and then reviewed for accuracy by paleontologists Dr. Jason Dunlop, Dr. Peter Van Roy and Dr. Tom Hegna. We thank them for their time and expertise.

GLOSSARY

adaptation: a change that helps an organism become better suited to its environment. Usually, when adaptation happens, the organism's DNA changes.

appendage: a body part that sticks out, like a leg or antenna

arthropod: an animal that has a segmented body, jointed appendages and an external skeleton. Members of the arthropod family include crustaceans, insects, millipedes and arachnids.

bottom-feeder: an animal that finds food on the ocean floor

deoxyribonucleic acid (DNA): the microscopic material found in cells that carries the genetic information for an organism

era: a major division of geologic time, divided into periods

fossil: an impression made in stone of a prehistoric animal or plant

gigantism: development to an unusually large size

invertebrate: an animal without a backbone

molt: to shed an external skeleton in order for an animal to grow

mutation: a sudden change in the structure of DNA

organism: a living thing that can grow and reproduce

paleontologist: a scientist who studies extinct animals and plants, and their fossils

period: a subdivision of an era

predator: an animal that hunts for other living animals (prey) to eat

radiometric dating: a scientific method for figuring out the age of rocks and other materials by measuring amounts of radioactivity in a sample

scavenger: an animal that eats whatever it finds, usually pieces of dead plants or animals

taxonomy: the classification of plants and animals according to shared traits

telson: the last element on the body or tail of some animals

vertebrate: an animal with a backbone

FURTHER READING

Books

Bugs Before Time: Prehistoric Insects and Their Relatives, by Cathy Camper. New York: Simon & Schuster Books for Young Readers, 2002.

Paleo Bugs: Survival of the Creepiest, by Timothy J. Bradley. San Francisco: Chronicle Books, 2008.

Online Resources

Eons, "The Age of Giant Insects," by PBS, 2017. www.pbs.org/video/the-age-of-giant-insects-mn9nez

"Big, Big Bugs," by Danika Painter. Arizona State University School of Life Sciences, Ask A Biologist, 2012. https://askabiologist.asu.edu/explore/prehistoric-insects

INDEX